AUTUMN I
BY
KEITH OGDEN

Autumn Leaves

A BOOK OF POETRY

KEITH OGDEN

Grafted

Copyright ©2010 Keith Ogden

The right of Keith Ogden to be identified as author of this work has been asserted by him.

First published 2010

All rights reserved

No part of this publication may be reproduced or transmitted in any form or by any means electronic or mechanical, including photocopy, recording, or any information storage and retrieval system, without permission in writing from the author.

All scripture quotations are from the Amplified Bible unless otherwise stated.

Published in Great Britain by

Grafted

www.graftedbydesign.co.uk

ISBN 978-0-9562603-3-8

CONTENTS

Introduction

1 New Beginnings
2 Peace from Me to You
3 God's Love
4 Why Lord Did You Come?
5 Something Beautiful
6 Precious as Gold
7 Hidden Treasures
8 Forgiveness
9 Two Hearts
10 Branches of Love
11 Dreaming of You
12 Which Way?
13 Candles
14 Dedicate
15 The Future
16 Faithful God
17 A True Friend
18 New Life

I thank the Lord who hears and answers prayer and gives us the desires of our hearts.
Psalm 103

Introduction

For years, I have enjoyed writing both poetry and songs which most have been given to individuals and churches.

This has been over a period of over 40 years.

I dedicate these poems to my best friend.

The subject of relationships is available in my third book, The Affairs of the Heart.

Marriage and right relationships are of God. They do play an important and caring role in today's society. The Bible is quite clear in that we can`t just please ourselves and have any kind of relationship as and when we choose.

I pray you will be both blessed and inspired as to what God has done and can do in all our lives as we walk close to Him and be obedient.

New Beginnings

Have you ever walked through the woods amongst the leaves?
Many thoughts, in and out, constantly weaves;
Wishing that you were no longer alone
With family & friends, but not the same.

It seems like the cold winter, bitter and strong
Has entered my heart forever and ever so long;
You breathe in the sharp fresh air and gasp
Will the day come no longer alone at last?

I look around at the beauty of what God has made
I want to give my whole to Him, almost to be sharp as a grass blade;
The snow covers the ground, two feet tall
I tell the Lord my all in all.

The Lord has blessed me that is true indeed
For my family and friends, but there is still a need;
I no longer wish to be like a lonely leaf
Blown around still with that little lonely grief.

My desire is always to please the Lord
For my life to be complete, away from that lonely road;
My confidence and rest in Jesus is true
I say Lord, who is else is like you?

Your word says, you satisfy my desires with good things
So that my youth is renewed on eagles' wings;
Father, your timing is perfect, this I know
I commit my ways to you, you're never too slow.

Peace from Me to You

Peace is flowing like a river, even in my heart
My love for you will never ever depart;
The love I have was given by the Lord
Your love pierced my heart, just like a sword.

Since I met you, you have brought me hope
Your tender touch, how real it is;
Your love is so real, deep within
Well and truly you are under my skin.

You inspire me, bless me every single day
What would I do without you, I will always say;
You are an answer to prayer, you bring me peace
Whenever I`m with you, I always feel at ease.

I long for the day when we will always be together
Being as one, with the sweet fragrance of heather;
I have opened my heart to you, unconditional
You bring peace to me, my beating heart still.

I think of you throughout each day
Will you be with me and forever stay?
I will always be there just for you
To protect, respect always loving you.

You are the woman of my dreams
For an eternity I waited, so it seems;
The Lord gives us the peace that forever stands
As we walk together, footprints along the sands.

I will care for you as you care for me
Whatever comes along, as one are we;
 Always in the Lord we stand together
You will always be mine alone forever.

3.

God`s Love

There was a time when I thought I was OK
Walking merrily along, not a care in the world;
Little did I know I was walking in sin?
That Jesus died to bring His peace within

The golden leaves had healing all around
Because I was empty, there was no sound;
Like a beating drum but without the sticks
Perhaps my mind was really playing tricks

Jesus came with healing in His wings
He is the only one in my heart sings;
Come to Him and you will find
Love Joy and peace, not the human kind

God`s love how great can it be
He sent his Son just for you and me;
He is so wonderful such a caring God
Give your cares to Him, every single load

As the leaves dance merrily around in the wind
So light is now my heart, He has forgiven my sins;
Perfect peace now rules in my heart
It`s a new life in Him, just the start

The air is crisp quiet; you can hardly hear a thing
There`s a sound within, the Spirit just quietly mingling;
I walk alone along this cold autumn time path
Come the summer, I jump and laugh!

4.
Why Lord Did You Come?

It is marvellous, just to know we were created
Not the story of evolution, which I always hated:
We were without hope and quite lost
Nowhere to go, just well and truly lost.

I am sure we could manage, just keep our heads low
No one can tell me or even where to go;
I was the captain of my ship, thanks
Doing quite well, high in the ranks.

Enjoying myself, just give me plenty of room
Trouble was, my life had this massive vacuum;
Nothing could fill it whatever I tried
I didn`t realise for me Christ died.

God so loved the world, so we read
Without His life we are dead indeed;
He is our hope if we trust in Him
So get real and don`t live in sin.

That`s why Lord you came for me
To shed your precious blood on Calvary;
Oh the love that drew salvations plan
Oh that mighty gulf God did span.

So Lord I now know why you came
It was pure real love, never any fame;
Jesus is the answer, my friend indeed
He is our whole in every need.

5. SOMETHING BEAUTIFUL

JUST WALK WITH ME NOW PAST THE AUTUMN TREES
BREATHE IN THE AIR AND FEEL IMMEDIATE RELEASE
LOOK AROUND AT THE DEEP BLUE SKY
FEEL THE GRASS LET HIM LIFT YOU HIGH.

HE IS A BREATH OF FRESH AIR, ALIVE AND ACTIVE
RUNNING THROUGH MY VEINS, IN HIM WE LIVE;
WE HAVE OUR BEING, OUR VERY SOUL
JESUS IN THE ONE TO MAKE YOU WHOLE

HE IS BEAUTIFUL WITH LOVE AND COMPASSION
THE ROSE OF SHARON, ABIDE IN ME,
IN HIM WE LIVE AND MOVE, OUR BEING
HE PUTS A SONG IN MY HEART, SO WE SING

JESUS TAKES THAT WHICH SEEMS IMPOSSIBLE
AND THROUGH HIS GRACE INTO THE
PLAUSIBLE;
HE TURNS ASHES INTO HIS BEAUTY
CHANGED INTO HIS GLORY DAY BY DAY

WE HAVE A GOD WHO CAN DO MIGHTY
THINGS
SO PUT YOUR HAND IN HIS, TAKE AWAY THE
STINGS
PEACE AT LAST HE WILL TAKE YOU HOME
MANSIONS THAT ARE MANY, IN HEAVEN WE
ROAM

EVERLASTING LIFE IS FOR THOSE WHO
BELIEVE
HE DIED ON THE CROSS TO BRING YOU
RELIEVE,
ALIVE IN CHRIST NEVER THE SAME AGAIN
SOMETHING BEAUTIFUL, IN HIM IT IS JUST
GAIN

6. Precious as Gold

Precious as gold are you and me
Hidden treasures in Christ have we,
Unfolding each day as we walk with Him
Abide in Christ you can only really win

It is a thing most wonderful, everlasting peace
Let it rule in your heart, accept that release,
Jesus is always the same, never any change
He is your friend, does not act strange

Commit your ways unto the Lord
You`ll never stray or go down the wrong road,
As long as you keep your eyes on Him
You won`t go wrong or walk in sin

He died for you, shed his precious blood
Claim it right now the devil withstood,
Victory is yours, just take it right now
Claim the word ,don`t work out how

Let His death really mean something to you
Walk in it accept it by faith, Him and just you;
It is something very precious never fades
You are precious like gold, never fades

We see things around us, and have desires
Are they really lasting, or like worn tyres?
Here today, and gone tomorrow
The things of this world just bring you sorrow

Precious as gold that life in you
Everlasting, forever, why feel blue?
He is the great I am, yesterday and today
He is your friend forever to stay

7. HIDDEN TREASURES

HAVE YOU EVER THOUGHT AS YOU GO ALONG?
WHAT IT WOULD BE LIKE FEELING WRONG;
WHAT I MEAN BY THAT, YOU DON`T FEEL RIGHT
SOMETHING MISSING DAY AND NIGHT

YOUR LIFE SO EMPTY, WITHOUT ANY HOPE
WHERE ARE YOU GOING, WHERE IS YOUR SCOPE?
JUST EXACTLY WHAT ARE YOU DOING?
LIFE IS SO EMPTY AND LIES IN RUINS

PEOPLE FILL THEIR LIVES WITH SO MANY THINGS
THEY DON`T LAST VERY LONG, MONEY AND GOLD RINGS;
TREASURES LAY UP FOR A BETTER DAY
TROUBLE IS, IT WILL NEVER STAY

POP STARS, CELEBRITIES ALL HAVE THEIR THING
CARS, HOUSES AND THE WELL KNOWN BLING;
BUT DOES IT REALLY LAST AND GIVE YOU PEACE
WHY DO YOU GO WITH THEM IN THE WRONG RACE?

AUTUMN LEAVES, ALL AROUND AS WE WALK
ALL DRIED UP THE COLOURS ARE, CRUMBLES LIKE CHALK;
NEW BEGINNINGS A FUTURE LIFE
JUST AROUND THE CORNER, EVERLASTING LIFE

THE DUST FLARES UP, JUST LIKE A MIST
CAN`T SEE A THING BEYOND MY WRIST;
WHICH PATH I TAKE, I DO NOT KNOW
WHERE IS THE TREASURE, WHERE IS THE GLOW?

HIDDEN TREASURES IN CHRIST CAN BE FOUND
HE IS SOLID, FEET FIRM ON THE GROUND;
TREASURES EVERLASTING THAT DON`T DISAPPEAR
REACH OUT RIGHT NOW TO TAKE AWAY ALL FEAR

8. *Forgiveness*

Is it not a wonderful thing what God has done
Whilst we walked in sin He sent His only Son?
Without hope, lost and had gone astray
He sent Jesus to show us the only way

Oh the love that drew salvations plan and grace
Perhaps one day we will understand in that heavenly place;
His forgiveness is beyond all comprehension
His name is the only thing to mention

A voice in heaven one day did say
Who will go who can I send?
Jesus responded here I am Lord
Send me I will go to put sin to an end

He came, was born very lowly
Nowhere special yet so holy;
He walked amongst us healed so many
His love was free, plentiful for any

Amazing grace was the greatest price
He never gave a thought, not even twice;
Freely He gave His life for you and me
Forgiveness always there to set us free

If you believe in Jesus you are free indeed
From all sin, sickness and disease
Eternal life is yours to claim
Call right now upon His mighty name

Forgiveness is always there at any time
Call upon the Lord cry unto Him
He is worthy to be praised at all times
He forgives us all and all our crimes

9. Two Hearts

When two hearts drift away they are no longer one
Yours and mine whatever went wrong?
My love for you never waned
I searched for you again always strained

I will never let you go always be there
All you have to do is turn and know where
I am not far off and watch over you
Let your heart and mine again be as one

I gave my heart for you laid it down
Became part of you forever known
Let me again be in your heart
I love you more as a whole, not just a part

If you only knew what you meant to me
I am too scared to say, in case you flee
I long for the day when together we are
In each other's arms, you are my star

Please give me a chance that is all I ask
To prove my love for you is no small task
My heart yearns and cries after you
Only you alone my love are true

Two hearts beat together as one
No longer alone, forever as one
My love for you is forever strong
You are my theme of my song

Two hearts come together at long last
The hurts and sorrow a thing of the past
Together we walk hand in hand
Just like the two in the sand

10. Branches of Love

I am the vine, Jesus has said
Without me the branch is as good as dead
My Father is the true vinedresser
Anything else really is so much lesser

You are cleansed, purified because of the word
My word is sharper than any two edged sword
If you abide in me and I in you
Great things, I promise you will do

Dwell in me, I will dwell in you
Everything else just is not true
Follow me the branch of love
Soar like an eagle to the heavens above

On eagles wings He bears me up
Soaring higher up and up
His love for me never ever ends
Only grows daily, His love He sends

He reaches out for you and me
Just like branches of a young tree
Peace like a river flows in my heart
Like He said, I will never depart

So don`t think that you`re ever alone
Being part of Him being as one
His love forever He does send
A love everlasting never to end

The branch of love where is it now
It is within myself and does grow
Jesus is that true vine
His care for me so divine

11. Dreaming of You

Wow you won't believe who I dreamt of last night
The girl of my dreams, you bet, that's right
She was there, right there as plain as could be
Walking, talking such a reality

I couldn't believe it when she came up to me
I thought I was dreaming, if that could be
My heart never stopped beating as fast as it did
Almost like a tin it blew off the lid

She was so real uncanny and true
Never a dull moment, the sky so blue
We walked by the river hand in hand
Music to my ears more like a band

I mean, how such a thing like this can ever happen
My heart didn't skip a beat, but more like ten
How do I get this dream to become real?
I know I will tell her how I really feel

Dreaming of being with you, more like heaven
I'll stay up there forever to be with you
But when I wake up it's back down to earth
Even more determined to give this dream birth

Dare I risk saying something now?
Or will she kick me over the hill and brow
Perhaps I'll end up a night on the river
Me and my big mouth do not but shiver

Oh well back to reality I suppose
My dreams hopefully one day transpose
From one world to another it can only be
Me and my girl on the loved filled sea

Which Way?

That my friend is a very good question
Especially when I`ve got nothing left but me pension
I`m broke and skint nothing much to do
I`m on me own even got the flu

Well I once used to go to church every day
Then they kicked me out because I wouldn`t pay
Three times on Sunday, pensioners club too
Never tithed or paid me due

I thought I was religious by going to church
The preacher said I`m in the lurch
Said somat `bout going to hell
Nay lad me dad used to ring church bell

The congregation on a Sunday got less and less
Same boring stuff, couldn`t wait to play chess
Hymn, reading, hymn, notices and about next week
`Tis no wonder old roof had a leak

Guaranteed without fail, collection bag came round
Trouble were I didn`t even have a pound
Silent offering we were asked to give
It`s oreght for you, I need what bit I`ve got to live

It`s then an old friend called to see me one day
Said don`t worry lad you don`t have to pay
Somebody called Jesus paid the price
Give your life to Him and don`t think twice

It says in the Bible he is the way
There is no other, what else can I say
My life`s been better a 100 per cent
I can stand straight, no longer bent

My burdens are gone at Calvary
There He died for you and me
Said He had come to set us free
He is the way, now I can see!

Candles

Shadows, shadows are on the wall
Makes things taller down they fall
The candles burn, flames anew
Watch the light nothing to rue

A knock at the door, could that be her?
Something inside me starts to stir
I remember the last time she was here
The candles went out, she made me leer

I won't go into that right now
I'd better make them candles aglow
With the candles and open fire
Cosy as a cat I'll never tire

Tick tock the time goes by
Oh my goodness time will fly
Especially when she is in this place
Space and time has no pace

In each other's arms we just stare
Into each other`s eyes as much as I dare
We feel the comfort of each other
Candles flickering, but us forever

The next day you`re gone, and I`m alone
The candles gone out, why don`t you phone?
Did I say something, cause you upset
I am now worried and begin to fret

The candles when new look fresh and bright
Just like you, so beautiful and light
I hope one day you will return
To share a candle to see it burn

14. *Dedicate*

I give my life Lord wholly to you
Dedicate myself fully and true
The fields are white unto harvest and full
Hear and live, dedicate your whole

I hear the cry go forth and tell
Preach to the lost to save from hell
Heal the sick and demons cast out
In the name of Jesus be free, let it out

Why be afraid to proclaim His name
When Jesus is true forever the same?
Yesterday, today, tomorrow never changes
He is the solid the Rock of Ages

In today`s society we do our own thing
Go with the flow is something we all sing
Afraid to commit or to be true
Where do we go, what do we do?

The word dedicate I'd banded about
Like it was some common word to shout
Follow this and follow that
We`d all do well to leave that out

Call upon the Lord whilst He may be found
Cry out to Him on solid ground
Commit your life to Him without fail
The sting of death has no tail

So commit your ways unto the Lord
Don`t get things just to hoard
Build up treasures that will not perish
Serve in the Spirit and not the flesh

The Future

What will happen often we wonder?
Read the stars or we blunder
If I were you I'd leave them well alone
Read the word of God, trust in the one

Where do we come from, or where do we go
Wandering like a lost one no open door
Who do we trust in or we depend
Jesus is the one who knows our end

My times are in His hands the Bible says
So why do we worry and scurry along?
Our future in Him is only secure
Christ the solid rock, that's Him for sure

He holds my hand, Jesus holds my hand
Safely to Heaven He takes me there
A mansion prepared nothing but the best
In Jesus my Saviour I find rest

God has a good plan for you and me
I know for sure He set me free
He made me whole in word and deed
Gracious is He meets all my need

So won't you put your hand in His?
Why trust yourself to nothing less?
He gives us beauty for ashes so wonderful
I wait on you Lord, so rich so full

16. Faithful God

Faithful God the one I adore and praise
I close my eyes quietly before you
Feel your presence and all your ways
Surrounded with such a beautiful haze

You are here Lord even right now
Where in your presence I come and bow
Before your throne I do kneel
Your love to me you do reveal

Faithful one who never ever changes
Your beauty revealed throughout the ages
Creator of the world and the universe
Everlasting Father Prince of Peace

I can depend upon you Lord, at all times
There is no other that one fines
Trust in Him with all your heart
On his understanding never part

He sees into the future and our every need
Faithful to the end, in word and deed
From the very beginning to the end of time
I am His and He is mine

He knows us better than we know ourselves
Never leaves or forsakes us, no one else
My life is in Him, from beginning to end
The Alpha and Omega a real true friend

17.   ## A True Friend

Let`s face it, who are your friends?
Social websites, texts, never ends
Who do you rely on when the cards are down?
The one who loves you and gives an everlasting crown

Computer games of all different kinds
The kids are memorised going blind
Bang. Crash, Ouch! Comes from the screen
Are these true friends never seen?

T.V and mobiles fill our dreams
But in reality it`s not what it seems
Outdoor pursuits and many clubs
Fill our lives with false centred hubs

The friends we have even let us down
Say a wrong word or even a frown
Bang goes the door never turns around
Not a goodbye or any other sound

Maybe the Lord allows these kinds of trials
To test and see who else fails
At last to our senses we do come
When we turn to Jesus and come home

Make Him always your first port of call
Not the telephone or you might fall
Cast your cares on Him today
Jesus said He will never go away

Jesus I call on you right now
Hear my cry Lord wipe my brow
Take my tears wipe them Lord
In you my trust forever afford

18. New Life

It`s a new life we`ve only just begun
A new beginning, no end just real fun
A new season, the spring of life
Draw from the water that leads to eternal life

We`ve not come from a pond or even an ape
Created by the Lord of Heaven and Earth
Being changed daily in Christ alone
All because of Him and the new birth

Gone is the past, the old put away
My new nature in Christ is here to stay
I am no longer bound by sin
Jesus has set me free from within

I was once in darkness but now I`m free
Jesus has died for you and for me
He rose again on the third day
Gave us new life forever to stay

A new beginning, a chance of something new
Don`t dwell upon the past, He lives in you
Look to the future for a bright hope
He sees in you a great deal of scope

He has called you by name before you were born
Saved and healed you from all scorn
He can do that which is impossible
Bring about all that is possible

From dark unto light in a twinkle of an eye
We will be changed when we meet Him in the sky
Forever and ever in eternity
Praise and worship for setting us free